Level B Book 1

PUNCTUATION PUZZLER

COMMAS & MORE

SERIES TITLES

Commas & More	Run-Ons
Level A Book 1	Level A Book 1
Level B Book 1	Level B Book 1
Level C Book 1	Level C Book 1

D1607131

M.A. Hockett

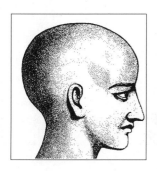

© 2002
THE CRITICAL THINKING COMPANY
www.CriticalThinking.com
P.O. Box 448 • Pacific Grove • CA 93950-0448
Phone 800-458-4849 • FAX 831-393-3277
ISBN 0-89455-815-3
Printed in the United States of America

To Mother,

See what you made me do? Thanks.

Edited by Christine Broz

TABLE OF CONTENTS

INTRODUCTION iv

Comma Series: What's What (Items in a Series) 1

Comma: Action (Phrases in a Series) 3

Comma: Who's Being Addressed (Noun of Address) 5

Comma: Separate State (City and State) 7

Comma: Addresses (Street, City, and State) 9

Comma: Around the Year (Month, Day, Year) 11

Comma: Special Beginnings (Introductory Words) 13

Comma: Who Says What (Dialogue) 15

Comma: Conjunctions—Tie It Up 19

Comma: Explain It (Nonessential Appositives) 22

Question Mark/Period: Questionable Endings 23

Exclamation Mark: Exclaimed or Not 25

Apostrophe: Leaving Out Letters (Contractions) 27

Apostrophe: Who's An Owner (Possessive) 28

Quotation Marks: Quote or Title? 32

SAMPLE LESSONS 34

ANSWER KEY 39

INTRODUCTION

Punctuation Puzzler gives practice in using context clues and reading comprehension to apply punctuation rules, as well as in carefully reading and following directions. The activities are based on the idea that punctuation is necessary to make written communication clear. Students must really *think,* using context clues for analyzing, comparing, contrasting, and deducing. Students must determine where to place punctuation so that the written form communicates the intended meaning.

> *My three cousins are Mary Sue George and Jerry Lee.*

The context clue *three cousins* tells us that the words *Mary Sue George* represent two people, so *Mary Sue* is one person. Put commas after *Sue* and *George.*

Punctuation Puzzler may be used for practice in applying rules in context or as part of a systematic program for developing punctuation and thinking skills. Each page includes the rule and instructions and can be used for independent practice. For students requiring instruction or remediation in grammar rules, you may want to use *The Language Mechanic*, also available from The Critical Thinking Company. For more practice applying punctuation in context, you may want to use *Editor in Chief.*®

Punctuation Puzzler's activity content is uniquely designed to facilitate the use of deductive reasoning in conjunction with the application of punctuation rules. It does so by presenting examples which portray distinct differences in meaning based on whether or not the rule is applied correctly. For example, notice how the meaning of the same words is affected when the placement of the punctuation is changed:

> *"Carly," says Jonny, "is a red-haired girl."*

> *Carly says, "Jonny is a red-haired girl."*

Punctuation Puzzler uses this concept to advantage. Students must use context clues that are sometimes embedded as information in the same sentence, sometimes given in an adjacent sentence, and sometimes indicated in pictures.

Writing time is at a minimum so students can concentrate on the reasoning. Typically, the activities require only editing, e.g., commas or other marks must be added in the correct place; however, you may want to extend the required activities to include more writing. Have students write their own sentences illustrating the correct application of the grammar rule.

For some students, it will be a new idea to look for subtle differences in context in order to decide how to punctuate. For those who need further guidance, see the Sample Lessons on page 34.

Comma Series: What's What

1. Which picture shows the meaning of the text if you must add three commas to correct it? Add the three commas where they belong.

    The things he likes to watch are girls TV stars and planets.

2. Use the picture to find the meaning of the text. Add two commas to correct it.

    The children could find only paper dolls and scissors in the cabinet. They left the dolls but used the other two things to make paper snowflakes.

3. Find the meaning of the text. Add three commas to correct it.

    Tommy Joe Sara Jeremy and Jane are out on the dance floor. They make two awesome couples.

RULE: In a series of three or more items, place a comma after each item except the last. *Mary Sue and Bob like bread, butter, and jam.*

Comma Series: What's What

4.   Use the picture to find the meaning of the text. Add the necessary
      commas.

> **At the party, the cakes were delicious! I had one
> piece of each type. There were angel food chocolate
> mint and peanut butter cakes. I was glad the angel
> food was plain.**

5.   The picture shows what you received. Find the meaning of the text. Add
      the necessary commas.

> **I ordered wax dummies and wigs for
> my wax museum. That dummy
> company got the order wrong. They
> sent wax dummies and wigs instead!
> The dummies were plastic. The wax
> was just a blob.**

6.   Find the meaning of the text. Add the necessary commas.

> **At the race, we watched both distance runners and
> sprinters. The results were posted in three columns.
> They showed distance runner and time.**

RULE: In a series of three or more items, place a comma after each item except
the last. *Mary Sue and Bob like bread, butter, and jam.*

Comma Series: Action

7.   Use the picture clues to find the meaning of the text. Add the necessary commas to correct it.

The girl will listen to the teacher eat her lunch and go to recess.

the girl   her teacher

8.   Use common sense to decide which picture shows something Jorge does. Add the necessary commas.

Jorge just got up. He'll make his bed wash his face and eat breakfast.

RULE: In a series of three or more items, place a comma after each item except the last. *She goes home, shuts the door, and reads a book.*

Comma Series: Action

9.   Find the meaning of the text. Add two commas to correct it.

**They'll color the snowman white out the mistakes
and hand it in.**

**We find the snow white out in the field brown on the
city streets and black by the smoky factories.**

10.   Find the meanings of the sentences. Add commas to correct them.

**He'll rub his head with the oil slick down his hair
and go. Then he'll arrive at the shore clean the oil
slick down at the beach and leave.**

RULE: In a series of three or more items, place a comma after each item except
the last. *She goes home, shuts the door, and reads a book.*

Comma: Who's Being Addressed

11. Which picture below shows the meaning of the text? Add one comma to correct it.

We have been studying Mr. Taylor. We've learned about the pyramids in your book, *Taylor's Egypt*.

12. Use the picture to find the meaning of the text. Add one comma to correct it.

We are on the case. We have been studying Mr. Goldstein. He is our chief suspect John.

Mr. Goldstein

13. a. Find the meaning of the text. Add one comma to correct it.

Kristen put the lights out. If you do as I say, you will lower your electric bill.

b. Find the meaning of the text. Add one comma to correct it.

Manuel put the lights out. Then, Amanda he scared us with his howling.

RULE: Use commas to set off a noun of address (the name of the person being spoken to). *Come here, Jo, right now.*

Comma: Who's Being Addressed

14.   Find the meaning of the text. Add two commas to correct it.

> **Sherry is running Sonia. Do you want to run with her?**

> **Sherry is running Arbuckle. I just hope that old dog doesn't have a heart attack Sonia.**

15.   Find the meaning of the text. Add the necessary comma.

> **You can come back out. The rain is over Johnny.**

> **It is sunny over everyone else, but the rain is over Harry.**

Harry

16.   Find the meaning of the text. Add the necessary commas.

> **We are really shaking Carly. She needs to wake up now!**

> **We are really shaking Kathy. You're sooo frightening! As if you could scare us!**

RULE: Use commas to set off a noun of address (the name of the person being spoken to). *Come here, Jo, right now.*

Comma: Separate State

17. Which picture helps illustrate one of the sentences? Add four commas to correct the paragraph.

I was telling Helena how great it is to live in Montana. She thought Aptos California was cooler than any town in Montana. I said "Billings Montana is really cool. So is every place in that state. Helena, Montana is a really cool state, especially in winter!"

18. Use the picture to help you find the meaning of the text. Add four commas to correct the sentences.

I was talking to Pierre. "Pierre, Nebraska and South Dakota will be on our tour. Pierre South Dakota is a capitol city. Lincoln Nebraska is another capitol city."

RULE: Use commas to set off the state IF it comes after a city and tells what state the city is in. *I'm in Macon, Georgia, now.* If the state name is used to begin a new thought, do NOT use a comma after the state. *John, Utah is not the "Show Me" state.*

Comma: Separate State

19.   Find the meaning of the text. Add any necessary commas.

**If your name is Beverly Hills, California is the place
you ought to be.**

**If you are in Los Angeles California is the place
crowded with movie stars?**

20.   Find the meaning of the text. Add any necessary commas.

**When you are in the city of New York, New York is
the state you're in. New York, New York includes
Manhattan Island.**

RULE: Use commas to set off the state IF it comes after a city and tells what
state the city is in. *I'm in Macon, Georgia, now.* If the state name is used to begin
a new thought, do NOT use a comma after the state. *John, Utah is not the "Show
Me" state.*

Comma: Addresses

21.   Use the picture to find the meaning of the text. Add two commas to
       correct the text.

> It's nice to live just a mile from the ocean! My cousin
> lives even closer, in the town of Beach Flats East. I'm
> at 45 Knowles Avenue Beach Flats West Virginia.

22.   Find the meaning of the text. Add two commas to correct it. (See the map
       above if needed for help.)

> I'm trying to find the house where I was born. This
> state is landlocked, but the mountains are very
> scenic. Well, here it is! I'm at 12 Mountain Road
> Hightown West Virginia.

23.   Find the meaning of the text. Add two commas to correct it.

> Georgia, New York will be a good place for
> sightseeing. Also, Georgia, I want to see "42nd Street"
> on Broadway. Let's meet at 213 West 42nd Street New
> York New York.

RULE: Use commas to separate the elements of an address within a sentence
when you have this format: street address, city, state (or district or country).

Comma: Addresses

24. Find the meaning of the text below. Add two commas.

I'll send the package of baseball cards from Park Road South to the north end of the road. The address is 42 Park Road North Bangor South Dakota.

25. Find the meaning of the text. Add the necessary commas.

I've met 32 Main Street residents, Washington, at 42 Park Place Drive Washington D.C.

26. Find the meaning of the text. Add the necessary commas.

Mary is in Poeville. She sent a birthday card to her cousin, who lives in the town to the north. She sends it to 45 Oak Way North Poeville California.

RULE: Use commas to separate the elements of an address within a sentence when you have this format: street address, city, state (or district or country).

Comma: Around the Year

27. Which picture shows a date mentioned in the text? Add one comma to correct the text.

> **We had a celebration on February 11 1950. On**
> **February 11, 1995 people joined us. That's almost**
> **2000 people!**

28. Find the meaning of the text. Add the missing comma to correct the sentences.

> **On July 4, 2002 there were only 1000 firecrackers.**
> **On the next July 4, 2005 firecrackers will go off all**
> **at the same time.**

29. Find the meaning of the text. Add a comma to correct the sentences.

> **On March 30, 2003 shoes were in her closet. As you**
> **can tell, at least one was missing its mate! On March**
> **31, 2002 she found three more shoes.**

RULE: Use commas to separate the year when given this format within a sentence: *month day year*. *On May 12, 1992, he was born.* If the number after the day is not the year for that day, do not use a comma. *On May 10, 400 teams competed.*

Comma: Around the Year

30.   Find the meaning of the text. Add any missing commas.

> **We have been working hard on our car design. By May 12 2500 flying cars will become a reality. In that same year, by June 1, 5000 cars will come off the assembly line. Over the next few weeks, that number will increase to 7000.**

31.   Find the meaning of the text. Add any missing commas.

> **On Wednesday, August 15 2025 personal space craft were sold. Therefore, we missed our goal of 3000 sales.**

32.   Find the meaning of the text. Add any missing commas.

> **On September 15 2025 thinking machines will be produced. I think there will be just a few. In 2030, five years later, the number produced may be up to 1000.**

RULE: Use commas to separate the year when given this format within a sentence: *month day year. On May 12, 1992, he was born.* If the number after the day is not the year for that day, do not use a comma. *On May 10, 400 teams competed.*

Comma: Special Beginnings

33.   Match each sentence below to the picture that shows its meaning. Write the correct letter in each blank.

My scales are rough, aren't they? ____

My, scales are rough, aren't they? ____

A.  My hand feels the scales.

B. Me

34.   The picture matches the meaning of only one of the underlined sentences. The other underlined sentence needs a comma. Add it where it belongs.

   a.   **Which is best for me, soda, water, or coffee?**

   Well water is probably the best of those.

   b.   **Should I drink tap, well, or bottled water?**

   Well water is probably the best of those.

RULE: Use a comma to set off an introductory word, such as *Yes, No, Well, My,* and *Maybe.* (Introductory words are found at the beginning of a sentence.) *Well, I guess I'm ready.*

Comma: Special Beginnings

35.   Find the meaning of the text. Add the missing comma where it belongs.

My two-year-old brother can be such a pain! Is yours?

Yes you got that right. *No* is one of the first words he learned.

36.   Find the meaning of the text. Add the missing comma where it belongs.

We'd better keep the baby healthy.

Well that's true. Well babies grow into healthy kids like us.

37.   Find the meaning of the text. Add the missing commas where they belong.

Uh oh. He just fell on his nose! No bandages are available. Do you have an ice pack?

No I don't have one. Should we use a cherry popsicle?

Maybe but he likes grape better!

RULE: Use a comma to set off an introductory word, such as *Yes, No, Well, My,* and *Maybe*. (Introductory words are found at the beginning of a sentence.) *Well, I guess I'm ready.*

Comma: Who Says What

38.   Match each sentence to its picture. Write the correct letter in each blank.

"Hoppy," said Bartholomew, "is a strange frog."   ____

Hoppy said, "Bartholomew is a strange frog."   ____

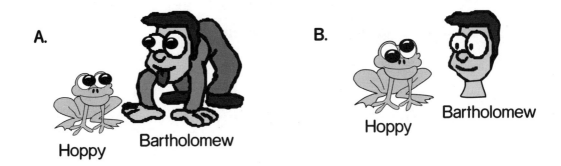

A.

Hoppy   Bartholomew

B.

Hoppy   Bartholomew

39.   Use the picture to find the meaning of the text. Add one set of quotation marks and a comma to correct it.

I said I really liked Mary, and I wanted to find out if
she liked me. I overheard Sidney saying
Mary likes me.

Me, after
hearing Sidney

RULE: Quotation marks enclose spoken words. Commas separate quotations from a speaker (the comma goes inside quotation marks before the speaker). *"Now,"* she said, *"go play."* Use no comma after an exclamation or question. *"Great!"* he yelled.

Comma: Who Says What

40. Find the meaning of the text. Add two sets of quotation marks and two commas to correct it.

Help me! my sister was yelling to get out of her bedroom cluttered with junk.

"No," our brother was yelling to get out of your bedroom is nearly impossible!

41. Find the meaning of the text. Add any quotation marks and commas needed to correct it.

The newborn baby screamed a whole lot.

"Does that hurt your ears? I asked his brother.

Answering, the brother screamed A whole lot!

42. Find the meaning of the first sentence. Add any quotation marks and commas needed to correct it.

The horse said Bobby is too slow for me.

The horse might tell us otherwise if she could talk.

RULE: Quotation marks enclose spoken words. Commas separate quotations from a speaker (the comma goes inside quotation marks before the speaker). *"Now," she said, "go play."* Use no comma after an exclamation or question. *"Great!" he yelled.*

Comma: Who Says What

43.   Find the meaning of the text and add the necessary punctuation.

Gretchen said Paul has left her boyfriend.

I said I'm sorry to hear that, Paul.

44.   Find the meaning of the text and add the necessary punctuation.

I asked if the boys were in the bathtub.

**He asked If the boys were in the bathtub, wouldn't it
be fun to steal their towels?**

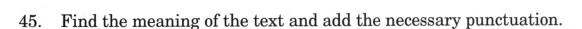

45.   Find the meaning of the text and add the necessary punctuation.

I shouted Marla's last name to him.

I shouted Marla's last name is Jones!

RULE: Quotation marks enclose spoken words. Commas separate
quotations from a speaker (the comma goes inside quotation marks before
the speaker). *"Now," she said, "go play."* Use no comma after an
exclamation or question. *"Great!" he yelled.*

17

Comma: Who Says What

46.   Find the meaning of the text and add the needed punctuation.

   We did not like what he asked.

   We did not like what? he asked.

47.   Find the meaning of the text and decide which sentence has a quotation. Add quotation marks and a comma where they belong.

   I asked Gardenia how Ann felt about her. She said Ann is really mad at me.

   I asked Gardenia how Ann felt about me. She said Ann is really mad at me.

RULE: Quotation marks enclose spoken words. Commas separate quotations from a speaker (the comma goes inside quotation marks before the speaker). *"Now," she said, "go play."* Use no comma after an exclamation or question. *"Great!" he yelled.*

Comma: Conjunctions—Tie It Up

48. Which picture shows the meaning of the sentence if it is missing one comma? Correct the sentence.

The man was tall and skinny dogs sniffed at him.

49. The picture below shows the meaning of the text. If a comma is needed, add it where it belongs.

We sell the necklace and the ladies' watch.
Only the buyer can see us.

50. Find the meaning of the text. Add commas where they belong.

We sell the necklace and the ladies watch.
They are hoping for a cheaper necklace but
this is our last item.

RULE: Use a comma to separate independent clauses joined by a conjunction, such as *or, and*, or *but*. *We yelled, but they left.* (An independent clause has both subject and verb.)

Comma: Conjunctions—Tie It Up

51.   Use the picture to help you find the meaning. Add any necessary comma.

The owners take off the collars and the dogs run.

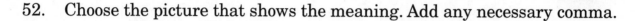

52.   Choose the picture that shows the meaning. Add any necessary comma.

They take off the collar and the dog's tag. The dog never wakes up!

53.   Find the meaning of the text. Add the one missing comma.

We found all the pencils but two were broken. We'd have to replace those two.

We found that all the tools but two were broken. We kept those two good ones.

54.   Read the text below. Add any needed commas.

The girls will dump the orange boots and will pick up green socks at the costume shop. They choose the masks and Will picks the rubber noses.

RULE: Use a comma to separate independent clauses joined by a conjunction, such as *or, and,* or *but. We yelled, but they left.* (An independent clause has both subject and verb.)

Comma: Conjunctions—Tie It Up

55. Find the meaning of the text. Correct it with one comma.

> **The queen begins the spring garden ceremony. She selects a bulb and the others plant it.**

> **The two aliens show their homes. We see the one's star and the other's planet.**

56. Find the meaning of the text. Correct it with one comma.

> **When do we get rid of our wood furniture?
> The oak goes now and the maple leaves later.**

> **We will put off cleaning the yard. We will rake all the oak leaves and the maple leaves later.**

57. Read and correct the sentences as necessary.

> **Earlier, they read the book but were tired. Now we read the book but we're bored.**

58. Read and correct the sentences as necessary.

> **Take a look at the car and its headlights up in the distance.**

> **See the spaceship. Its tail blinks and its head lights up in the distance.**

RULE: Use a comma to separate independent clauses joined by a conjunction, such as *or, and*, or *but. We yelled, but they left.*
(An independent clause has both subject and verb.)

Comma: Explain It

59.   Which picture shows Grandma? Add one comma to correct the text.

**Grandma, the monkey is hanging upside down. It hangs
by its tail a long attachment.**

60.   Use the picture to find the meaning. Add two commas to correct the text.

Watch out! Mrs. Greenfield the old bat is after you!

**You trampled those flowers, Mrs. Greenfield's pride and
joy.**

What we think of Mrs.
Greenfield!

61.   Find the meaning of the text. Add one comma to correct it.

I got my brother a big surprise. It was a new cell phone.

**I thought I'd get a new brother. Instead, I got a sister a big
surprise.**

RULE: Use commas to set off nonessential words of explanation
(appositives). *John, my best friend, is moving away.* (A nonessential
appositive is one that can be removed without a significant change in
meaning.)

Question Mark/Period: Questionable Endings

62.   Which picture shows the meaning of the text? Add punctuation to correct the text.

How is the boy flying the hoverboard

That should answer your question

How many hovering tricks did you show him

63.   Use the picture to find the meaning of the text. Add the necessary punctuation.

February is the month when you pick our spring clothes, Dad   May we pick our summer clothes In August, maybe we will pick fall clothes together.

RULE: Use a question mark to end a question. *May I go?* Use a period to end a statement. *You may go.*

Question Mark/Period: Questionable Endings

64.   Find the meaning of the text. Add ending punctuation as needed.

**When we have guests over, do the desserts last
That way, they'll be sure to eat the main course.**

**When we have guests over, do the desserts last
If not, remember to make more next time**

65a.   Find the meaning of the text. Add ending punctuation as needed.

**Will the operas sound much better than last year
If not, I would rather stay home and listen to the dog
howl.**

  b.   Find the meaning of the text. Add ending punctuation as needed.

**Will, the operas sound better than last year
If they didn't, I would use my earplugs and read my
book instead**

66.   Find the meaning of the text. Add ending punctuation as needed.

**Do your brothers work
If the answer is no, you will have to do your brothers'
work**

RULE: Use a question mark to end a question. *May I go?* Use a period to
end a statement. *You may go.*

Exclamation Mark: Exclaimed or Not

67.   Use the mood of each speaker to decide on ending punctuation. Add ending punctuation to each sentence.

   Tom (excited): Let's go see Liz wrestle that troll

   Earl (bored): Go see it yourself

   Lenny (scared): The trolls are coming here

   Chloe (disbelieving): Sure, they're coming

68.   Add correct punctuation inside the closing quotation marks.

   Without interest, Daryll read, "The tornado appeared suddenly from nowhere and picked up the whole house "

69.   Use the picture to help you find the meaning. Use correct ending punctuation.

   Are you taking me to the rally tonight?
   I can't wait to see the monster trucks

RULE: Use an exclamation mark to end a statement of enthusiasm, excitement, or fear. *I can't wait any longer!* Use a period to end a statement. *I can't wait any longer.* (Use context to decide.)

Exclamation Mark: Exclaimed or Not

70. Find the meaning of the text. Add one question mark, one exclamation mark, and one period where they belong. The picture illustrates *c* only.

a. **If we win the lottery, we each get mucho bucks. What excitement**

b. **You say there's a lot of excitement going on down the street, but I can't see anything. What excitement**

c. **Oh boy, we get to hear another lecture. I think I'll take a nap. What excitement**

71. Find the meaning of the text. Add correct ending punctuation.

Did you really sneak out during Aunt Maude's visit? How rude that was

I didn't know it was rude to sneak out. How rude was that

RULE: Use an exclamation mark to end a statement of enthusiasm, excitement, or fear. *I can't wait any longer!* Use a period to end a statement. *I can't wait any longer.* (Use context to decide.)

Apostrophe: Leaving Out Letters

72. Find the meaning of the text. Add an apostrophe where it belongs.

Im a pig owner. Ima Pig is the name of my pet.

73. Find the meaning of the text. Add an apostrophe where it belongs.

Well give you our best video games.

Well, give them to us now!

74. Find the meaning of the text. Add any missing apostrophes.

Jacob Weve, the stunt flyer, is coming! Weve has got to get ready to fly. Hes letting us take his picture first. Weve got to get ready for him!

75. Find the meaning of the text. Add any missing apostrophes.

We know Eileen Shed, the owner of the skate park. Shed let us in for free if we asked!

RULE: Use an apostrophe to show where letters are left out of a contraction. *don't = do not.*

Apostrophe: Who's An Owner 1

76.   Use the picture to find the meaning of the underlined sentence. Add one
      apostrophe to correct it.

**She watches as her sisters skate down the hill.
Oops! One of them loses a skate. <u>She finds and
carries her sisters skate down the hill.</u>**

77.   Find the meaning of the text. Add one apostrophe to correct the sentence.

**My aunts children are my cousins John and Paul.
She lets them host their own website.**

RULE: Add *'s* to make a singular noun possessive. *the dog's fur*

Apostrophe: Who's An Owner 1

78. Find the meaning and add the missing apostrophe.

> **The boys bat flies because they have no mosquitoes to practice on.**

> **The boys bat flies because he swings it too hard and loses control!**

79. Find the meaning and add the missing apostrophe.

> **I come out to watch my friends paint over the wall. They are covering it well. I go back inside to watch my uncles TV over his kitchen table.**

RULE: Add *'s* to make a singular noun possessive. *the dog's fur*

Apostrophe: Who's An Owner 2

80.   Use common sense to decide which picture shows the meaning of the
      text. Add the missing apostrophe.

      All of your sisters eyes are like yours.

81.   Use the picture and context to help you correct the sentences. Add an
      apostrophe to correct the sentences.

      **Terry loves his friends skateboards. Each friend has a
      board that is really fast.**

82.   Find the meaning of the text. Add two apostrophes to correct it.

      **At the wedding, there were beautiful flower
      arrangements of roses and babys breaths. Too
      bad I had to leave early with the two sick babies.
      They just spit up again. Boy, these babies breaths
      are stinky!**

RULE: To make a plural noun (ending in *s*) possessive, add an
appostrophe. *those kids' noses*
Add *'s* to make a singular noun possessive. *the dog's fur*

Apostrophe: Who's An Owner 2

83.   Which picture shows the meaning of the text? Add two apostrophes to correct the text.

That cats claws are sharp. Those claws points can dig in!

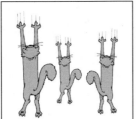 

84.   Find the meaning of the text. Add the missing apostrophe.

The baseball players field drives. They do it well because the field they field on feels fairly flat. I can't field balls in our park. It's too bumpy to catch even the balls right off the bat. Our baseball players field drives me crazy.

85.   Find the meaning of the text. Add punctuation to correct it.

I see those squirrels nest. It has pictures hung around the inside edges. I thought they were the familys portraits, but now I see they are just nuts.

RULE: To make a plural noun (ending in *s*) possessive, add an apostrophe. *those kids' noses*
Add *'s* to make a singular noun possessive. *the dog's fur*

Quotation Marks: Quote or Title?

86. Which picture shows the meaning of the first sentence? Add one pair of quotation marks to correct the text.

> **Apples is a visual treat. The color is good, and the lines are neat.**

> **Bananas are a tasty treat. When I view art, they're good to eat!**

87. Use the picture to help find the meaning. Add quotation marks.

> **Caroline is a fine example of a girl, but she's not inclined to spend her time in the modern art world.**

> **Emeline is a fine example of Impressionism, but I prefer the "Odyssey," as it's based on realism.**

∘ Emeline ∘

RULE: Enclose titles of poems, songs, stories, and works of art with quotation marks. *We loved hearing "The Little Mutt."*

Quotation Marks: Quote or Title?

88.   Find the meaning of the text. Add the missing quotation marks.

> **Let's discuss our preferences over drinks. Hot chocolate is my favorite. Other drinks are okay, but this one is outstanding. It inspired Ricky to sing Hot Chocolate on karaoke night.**

89.   Only one sentence below contains a quotation. Add a comma to separate the quotation from the speaker.

> **Shanya read "The Rhino Blows His Own Horn," a poem about an overconfident rhinoceros.**
>
> **Clarence said "The audience thought the rhino was too conceited."**

90.   Find the meaning of the text. Add the necessary quotation marks and commas to correct it.

> **He wondered what she was doing next. She said Dancing was what she would do next.**
>
> **I thought you were going to do another song he said.**
>
> **I am she said. I just told you the title.**

RULE: Enclose titles of poems, songs, stories, and works of art with quotation marks. *We loved hearing "The Little Mutt."*

SAMPLE LESSONS

Some readers may already be good at picking up context clues that can result in unexpected meanings. Others may need warm-up lessons to help them tune in to the "twists and turns" they may miss.

This section includes samples lessons on how to do the thinking required in the activities. (See Table of Contents, page iii, for a list of rules.) As students gain experience, lessons may be unnecessary.

Each lesson should start with a review of the rule. Show students an example sentence that has an ambiguous meaning and ask them what they think is meant. Then, give students two alternative context clues. Have them apply each clue to the sentence and add punctuation that clarifies the meaning according to the clue. Later lessons are abbreviated; use the same procedure as in the first lessons.

In the lessons, **T** = teacher dialog and **S** = student response.

Comma: Items and Phrases in a Series (pp. 1–4)

Rule: In a series of three or more items, place a comma after each item except the last one. (NOTE: Activities ask for placement of a comma before the final item; however, some consider this comma optional. You may want to revise the dialog and exercises to accommodate this option.)

Remind students that items in a series can include phrases, not just single words. Write this sentence where all can see it:
Our three favorite kinds of cookies are peanut butter almond fudge and black walnut.

T: "Now listen to this sentence." (Read it.) "How can we decide whether and where to put commas?"
S: "We know there are three, so we have to use the series rule."

T: "Right. Do we know where to put the commas?
S: "No." (Some may say Yes and give opinions of the kinds of cookies.)
T: "What kinds of cookies could there be? Remember, we know there are three."
S: "Peanut, butter almond fudge, and black walnut"
"Peanut butter, almond fudge, and black walnut"
"Peanut butter almond, fudge, and black walnut"
T: "Now let's say we get this clue."
Add one more sentence: *Each kind has a different nut flavor.*
"Now can we tell where the commas go?"
S: "Yes! Separate the words *butter* and *almond*. That way, each type has a nut in it!"
T: "Okay."
Place commas as follows:
Our three favorite kinds of cookies are peanut butter, almond fudge, and black walnut.
Summarize as follows:
T: "In these activities, you will use thinking exercises to decide how to punctuate sentences. You will use different kinds of sentences and many different rules, but they will all require you to think about what is meant so you use commas correctly. You must read directions for each activity then be detectives to find clues in the text or pictures. Sometimes you will choose the picture that shows the meaning based on clues in the sentences. Then you punctuate to fix the sentences. Sometimes you will match sentences to the correct pictures. Sometimes you must decide how to punctuate by just reading the sentences. At the bottom of each page is the rule you will be focusing on.

Comma: Noun of Address (pp. 5–6)

Rule: Use commas to set off a noun of address (the name of the person being spoken to).

Write this sentence where all can see it: *Put the food on John to warm it up.* Tell them that the sentence may be missing some punctuation.

T: "Today you will practice what you know about using commas with a noun of address.

"First, I'm going to read you a sentence. Listen carefully and I'll ask a question afterwards.

"Put the food on John to warm it up.

"Can you tell me what the food will go on?"

S: "John."

"The stove."

"We can't tell."

Draw a rough stove with a figure putting food on it, or just describe as below:

T: "What if we were given a picture clue that showed John putting the food on a burner? This would tell us that the food goes on a stove. But why is the word *John* in the middle of the sentence?"

S: "Someone is telling him what to do."

T: "Yes, so the word *John* is a noun of address. What do we need in the sentence to show that this word is used as a noun of address?"

S: "Commas!"

T: "Okay, where do they go?"

S: "One comma before the name, and one after."

T: "Good. Let's read what the sentence says with a pause at each comma." (All read out loud.)

Change the sentence as follows: *Put the blindfold on John so he can't see. Then we'll lead John.*

T: "Now we still have *John* in the middle of a sentence. Is he the one being spoken to?"

S: "No."

T: "Why is the name there?"

S: "It shows who you should put the blindfold on."

T: "Should we set it off with commas?"

S: "No."

T: "Okay. In the next activities, you will use thinking exercises to decide how to punctuate sentences. Read directions for each activity then be detectives to find clues in the text or pictures. Sometimes you will choose the picture that shows the meaning and then use commas to fix the sentences. Sometimes you will match sentences to the correct pictures. Sometimes you must decide how to punctuate by just reading the sentences. At the bottom of each page is the rule you will be focusing on."

Comma: City and State (pp. 7–8)

Follow the format of the first lessons, using the information below.

Rule: Use commas to set off the state IF it comes after a city and tells what state the city is in. If the state name is used to begin a new thought, do NOT use a comma after the state. (*John, Utah is not the "Show Me" state.*)

Sentence: *Harrison Nebraska is where I want to live.*

Context Clues:

A: "It's the best state." The sentence must be about Nebraska, so *Harrison* is a noun of address. Place a comma only after Harrison.

B: "It's the best city in all of Nebraska." Harrison is a city in the state of Nebraska. Set Nebraska off with commas."

Comma: Street, City, and State (pp. 9–10)

Follow the format of the first lessons, using the information below:

Rule: Use commas to separate the

elements of an address within a sentence when you have this format: street address, town, state (or district or country).

Sentence: *I live at 45 Logger's Lane North Adams South Carolina.*

Context Clues:

A: "My town is a smaller version of Adams, the town to the south." Your town must be North Adams. Place commas after *Lane* and *Adams*.

B: "Logger's Lane South is the other end of my street. To the north is North Adams, a smaller version of my town." *North* must go with *Logger's Lane*. The town can't be North Adams, so it is Adams.

Note: Students must also know that there is no state named just Carolina.

Comma: Year (pp. 11–12)

Follow the format of the first lessons, using the information below.

Rule: Use commas to separate the year when given this format within a sentence: *month, day, year*. If the number after the day is not the year for that day, a comma may be unnecessary.

Sentence: *On September 22, 1900 people arrived from other countries.*

Context Clues:

A: "That was a lot of people for our little town!" 1900 is number of people; therefore, use no comma after the number.

B: "We don't know how many there were." 1900 is the year; therefore, use a comma before and after the 1900.

Comma: Introductory Words (pp. 13–14)

Follow the format of the first lessons, using the information below:

Rule: Use a comma to set off an introductory word, such as *Yes, No,* and *Well*. (Introductory words are found at the beginning of a sentence.)

Sentence: *No I cannot spell.*

Context Clues:

A: "I hope that answers your question." Since *No* is an answer and is therefore used as an introductory word, it should be followed by a comma.

B: "I can spell all the other words, but not the word *No*." *No* refers to a word you cannot spell. Since it is not used as an introductory word, do not use a comma.

Comma: Dialogue—Quotation Marks (pp. 15–18)

Follow the format of the first lessons, using the information below:

Rule: Quotation marks enclose spoken words. Commas separate quotations from a speaker (comma goes inside quotation marks before the speaker). Use no comma after an exclamation or question.

Sentence: *Joy says I'm cold.*

Context Clues:

A: "She can't stop shivering." Since *Joy* is the one who is cold, she must be saying the words, "I'm cold." Therefore, use a comma after *says* and put quotation marks around *I'm cold*.

B: "She's feeling my forehead." Since *I'm* the one who's cold, I'm not using the actual words Joy said. Therefore, use no commas.

Comma: Conjunction (pp. 19–21)

Follow the format of the first lessons, using the information below:

Rule: Use a comma to separate independent clauses joined by a conjunction such as *or, and,* or *but*. (An independent clause has both subject and verb.)

Sentence: *Kari eats her breakfast and her egg rolls off the plate.*

Context Clues:

A: "She loves those egg rolls!" The word *rolls* is a noun; *egg* tells what kind of rolls. Kari is eating both her breakfast and her egg rolls. There is no need for a comma.

B: "That egg doesn't roll far!" (OR a simple sketch of an egg rolling off the plate.)
The egg is doing something, so *egg* is the subject and *rolls* is the verb. The independent clause, *her egg rolls off her plate*, is joined to the previous independent clause, *Kari eats her breakfast,* by the conjunction *and*. Use a comma before *and*.

Comma: Nonessential Appositives (p. 22)

Follow the format of the first lessons, using the information below.
Rule: Use commas to set off nonessential words of explanation (appositives). (A nonessential appositive is one that can be removed without a significant change in meaning.)
Sentence: *Herman, the worm is round and squishy.*
Context Clues:
A: "Do you see him, Herman?" You are speaking to Herman, so *the worm* is not used as an appositive. There is no need for another comma.
B: "Herman is my worm, and he's the only Herman we know." Herman is the worm so *the worm* is extra information about Herman. Use a comma after *worm*.

Question Mark/Period (pp. 23–24)

Follow the format of the first lessons, using the information below:
Rule: Use a question mark to end a question. Use a period to end a statement.
Sentence: *Can workers stand for many hours*
Context Clues:
A: "Those people making cans must get tired."

Can is used to describe what kind of workers. A statement is made, so use a period at the end.

B: "I especially want to know if the fruit pickers can stand for a long time." *Can* is not used to describe the type of workers. Also, the writer is wanting to know something. A question is asked, so put a question mark at the end.

Exclamation Mark (pp. 25–26)

Follow the format of the first lessons, using the information below:
Rule: Use an exclamation mark to end a statement of enthusiasm, excitement, or fear. Use a period to end a statement.
Sentence: *It's on fire*
Context Clues:
A: "I put the log in the fire. I expected it to catch fire." Nothing unusual is happening, so there's no reason to believe you are very emotional. No exclamation is made, so use a period at the end.
B: "We need to get out of here fast because the house is burning down!" You are excited and afraid, so the statement is an exclamation. Put an exclamation mark at the end.

Apostrophe: Contraction (p. 27)

Follow the format of the first lessons, using the information below:
Rule: Use an apostrophe to show where letters are left out of a contraction.
Sentence: *Bob and John said to Jo, "Well get to work!"*
Note: You may want to discuss the idea that other punctuation, if given correctly, can be a clue to the meaning of a sentence. Here, you may have the students add the other missing punctuation (comma after introductory word *Well*) after they decide on the meaning.
Context Clues:
A: "Then Jo said, 'You can't make me!'" Bob and John must be telling Jo what

to do, so the introductory word *Well* makes sense. No apostrophe is needed, but put a comma after *Well*.

B: "Jo said, 'Thanks for doing the work for me!'"

Bob and John must be offering to do the work. *Well* must mean the contraction for *We will*. Add an apostrophe: *We'll*.

Apostrophe: Possessive Singular
(pp. 28–29)

Follow the format of the first lessons, using the information below:

Rule: Add *'s* to make a singular noun possessive.

Sentence: *He saw the birds nest in the barn.*

Context Clues:

A: "I thought they would nest in the tree." Since *nest* shows what they are doing, *birds* must be plural. No apostrophe is needed.

B: "Her nest was very large." *Nest* is used as a noun, and *her* must refer to the bird. Therefore, the nest belongs to the bird. Use an apostrophe for *bird's*.

Apostrophe: Possessive Plural
(pp. 30–31)

Follow the format of the first lessons, using the information below:

Rule: To make a plural noun (ending in *s*) possessive, add an apostrophe.

Sentence: *My brothers names are very formal.*

Context Clues:

A: "He wants to shorten his first, middle, and last names." *He* suggests brothers is singular. Add an apostrophe before the *s*.

B: "They all want us to use their nicknames." *They* must refer to brothers (plural). Add an apostrophe after the *s*.

Quotation Marks: Title
(pp. 32–33)

Follow the format of the first lessons, using the information below:

Rule: Enclose titles of poems, songs, stories, and works of art with quotation marks.

Sentence: *The girls fight over the store's newcomer. Each girl wants to take Reginald home with her.*

Context Clues:

A: "The art store's newest painting would look good on their walls." *Reginald* must be a work of art, so enclose it with quotation marks.

B: "He had told them he would help paint their walls." *Reginald* is the name of a person, so do not use quotation marks.

ANSWERS

Comma Series: What's What (pp. 1–2)

1. Since you add three commas, the correct picture shows both a TV and stars.

The things he likes to watch are girls, TV, stars, and planets.

2. The picture shows three kinds of things, and you are told to add two commas.

The children could find only paper, dolls, and scissors in the cabinet. They left the dolls but used the other two things to make paper snowflakes.

3. Two couples means there are four people. Combining the names *Tommy* and *Joe* as one person makes the most sense.

Tommy Joe, Sara, Jeremy, and Jane are out on the dance floor. They make two awesome couples.

4. Angel food is plain, so chocolate mint is one of the three kinds of cake.

At the party, the cakes were delicious! I had one piece of each type. There were angel food, chocolate mint, and peanut butter cakes. I was glad the angel food was plain.

5. Since the order was wrong, and it was wax *and* dummies and wigs that were sent, use commas in the third sentence.

I ordered wax dummies and wigs for my wax museum. That dummy company got the order wrong. They sent wax, dummies, and wigs instead! The dummies were plastic. The wax was just a blob.

6. The clue *both* tells us that there are two things in the first sentence. *Three columns* tells us there are three things in the second sentence.

At the race, we watched both distance runners and sprinters. The results were posted in three columns. They showed distance, runner, and time.

Comma Series: Action (pp. 3–4)

7. The teacher is a man, so listening to the *teacher eat her lunch* makes no sense.

The girl will listen to the teacher, eat her lunch, and go to recess.

8. The bed can't wash Jorge's face, so there are three actions in the second sentence.

Jorge just got up. He'll make his bed, wash his face, and eat breakfast.

9. In the given context, leaving *white* with *snowman* makes no sense.

They'll color the snowman, white out the mistakes, and hand it in.

Below, the context shows that *snow* and *white* should not be separated.

We find the snow white out in the field, brown on the city streets, and black by the smoky factories.

10. In sentence 1, *oil* is a noun and *slick* is a verb. In sentence 2, *slick* is a noun.

He'll rub his head with the oil, slick down his hair, and go. Then he'll arrive at the shore, clean the oil slick down at the beach, and leave.

Comma: Who's Being Addressed (pp. 5–6)

11. Sentence two suggests that we are addressing the author, Mr. Taylor.

We have been studying, Mr. Taylor. We've learned about the pyramids in your book, *Taylor's Egypt*.

12. We are talking about Mr. Goldstein in the third person *(He)*, so we must be studying Mr. Goldstein. *John* is the noun of address.

We are on the case. We have been studying Mr. Goldstein. He is our chief suspect, John.

13. a. Kristen is being addressed, since *you* is used in the second sentence.

Kristen, put the lights out. If you do as I say, you will lower your electric bill.

b. Manuel is spoken of in third person *(he)*. Amanda is the one being addressed.

Manuel put the lights out. Then, Amanda, he scared us with his howling.

14. Sonia is the one being addressed. Arbuckle is the dog being run by Sherry.

Sherry is running, Sonia. Do you want to run with her?

Sherry is running Arbuckle. I just hope that old dog doesn't have a heart attack, Sonia.

15. Johnny is being addressed in the first two sentences. The third sentence means that it's raining *on* Harry.

You can come back out. The rain is over, Johnny.

It is sunny over everyone else, but the rain is over Harry.

16. Carly is referred to in third person, so she is not addressed. Kathy is being addressed.

We are really shaking Carly. She needs to wake up now!

We are really shaking, Kathy. You're sooo frightening! As if you could scare us!

Comma: Separate State (pp. 7–8)

17. Helena is being addressed, so *Billings* must be a town or city. The last sentence is about the state, so Helena is the person being addressed, not a city.

I was telling Helena how great it is to live in Montana. She thought Aptos, California, was cooler than any town in Montana. I said, "Billings, Montana, is really cool. So is every place in that state. Helena, Montana is a really cool state, especially in winter!"

18. *Pierre* is a noun of address in sentence two. Context shows that Pierre is a city in sentence three; Lincoln is a city in sentence four.

I was talking to Pierre. "Pierre, Nebraska and South Dakota will be on our tour. Pierre, South Dakota, is a capitol city. Lincoln, Nebraska, is another capitol city."

19. *California* starts a new thought (the first six words are an introductory phrase, which is followed by a comma).

If your name is Beverly Hills, California is the place you ought to be.

Below, *California* shows the state Los Angeles is in.

If you're in Los Angeles, California, is the place crowded with movie stars?

20. In the first sentence, New York starts a new thought.

When you are in the city of New York, New York is the state you're in. New York, New York, includes Manhattan Island.

Comma: Addresses (pp. 9–10)

21. Since the location is near the ocean, the state is Virginia, not West Virginia.

It's nice to live just a mile from the ocean! My cousin lives even closer, in the town of Beach Flats East. I'm at 45 Knowles Avenue, Beach Flats West, Virginia.

22. The state is landlocked, so it doesn't border the ocean. It is West Virginia.

I'm trying to find the house where I was born. This state is landlocked, but the mountains are very scenic. Well, here it is! I'm at 12 Mountain Road, Hightown, West Virginia.

23. *Georgia* is a noun of address and *"42nd Street"* is a play, so no extra commas are needed in the first two sentences.

Georgia, New York will be a good place for sightseeing. Also, Georgia, I want to see "42nd Street" on Broadway. Let's meet at 213 West 42nd Street, New York, New York.

24. If this end is Park Road South, the north end is Park Road North. Dakota is not a state, so the state is South Dakota.

I'll send the package of baseball cards from Park Road South to the north end of the road. The address is 42 Park Road North, Bangor, South Dakota.

25. Context tells us the words *32 Main Street* is not part of an address. The first Washington is a noun of address. *D.C.* is a district.

I've met 32 Main Street residents, Washington, at 42 Park Place Drive, Washington, D.C.

26. *North* is part of the town name, since it's north of Poeville.

Mary is in Poeville. She sent a birthday card to her cousin, who lives in the town to the north. She sends it to 45 Oak Way, North Poeville, California.

Comma: Around the Year (pp. 11–12)

27. The only date is *1950*. *1995* is the number of people who came.

We had a celebration on February 11, 1950. On February 11, 1995 is the number of people who joined us. That's almost 2000 people!

28. *2005* tells how many firecrackers.

On July 4, 2002, there were only 1000 firecrackers. On the next July 4, 2005 firecrackers will go off all at the same time.

29. Since you can tell a shoe was missing its mate, *2003* is the number of shoes.

On March 30, 2003 shoes were in her closet. As you can tell, at least one was missing its mate! On March 31, 2002, she found three more shoes.

30. Sentence three refers to *that same year*, so *2500* is the year. *5000* is the number of cars.

We have been working hard on our car design. By May 12, 2500, flying cars will become a reality. In that same year, by June 1, 5000 cars will come off the assembly line. Over the next few weeks, that number will increase to 7000.

31. *Therefore* suggests that 2025 is the number of space craft.

On Wednesday, August 15, 2025 personal space craft were sold. Therefore, we missed our goal of 3000 sales.

32. 2025 must be the year, since 5 years later is 2030.

On September 15, 2025, thinking machines will be produced. I think there will be just a few. In 2030, five years later, the number produced may be up to 1000.

Comma: Special Beginnings (pp. 13–14)

33. *My* is possessive in sentence one, and introductory in sentence two.

My scales are rough, aren't they? <u>**B**</u>

My, scales are rough, aren't they? <u>**A**</u>

34. Well water is the type of water meant in b, so *Well* is an introductory word only in *a*.

a. Which is best for me, water, soda, or coffee?

<u>Well, water is probably the best of those.</u>

b. Should I drink tap, well, or bottled water?

<u>Well water is probably the best of those.</u>

35. *Yes* is an introductory word answering the question. *No* refers to the word *no* itself.

My two-year-old brother can be such a pain! Is yours?

Yes, you got that right. *No* is one of the first words he learned.

36. *Well* is an introductory word in the second sentence. In the third sentence, *well* is an adjective describing babies.

We'd better keep the baby healthy.

Well, that's true. Well babies grow into healthy kids like us.

37. The second *No* and *Maybe* both introduce ideas.

Uh oh. He just fell on his nose! No bandages are available. Do you have an ice pack?

No, I don't have one. Should we use a cherry popsicle?

Maybe, but he likes grape better!

Comma: Who Says What (pp. 15–18)

38. In sentence one, Bartholomew speaks about Hoppy.

"Hoppy," said Bartholomew, "is a strange frog." <u>**B**</u>

Hoppy said, "Bartholomew is a strange frog." <u>**A**</u>

39. Since the narrator is sad, *me* in sentence two must refer to Sidney.

I said I really liked Mary, and I wanted to find out if she liked me. I overheard Sidney saying, "Mary likes me."

40. *To get out* were not the words the sister was yelling. The brother was yelling them.

"Help me!" my sister was yelling to get out of her bedroom cluttered with junk.

"No," our brother was yelling, "to get out of your bedroom is nearly impossible!"

41. A newborn could not speak. The speaker is clear in sentence two. In sentence three, the brother's answer is *A whole lot*.

The newborn baby screamed a whole lot.

"Does that hurt your ears?" I asked his brother.

Answering, the brother screamed, "A whole lot!"

42. Since the horse can't talk, Bobby is the one speaking.

"The horse," said Bobby, "is too slow for me."

The horse might tell us otherwise if she could talk.

43. Since Paul is addressed in the second sentence, he must be the one speaking in the first sentence. Also, *her* most likely refers to Gretchen.

"Gretchen," said Paul, "has left her boyfriend."

I said, "I'm sorry to hear that, Paul."

44. The question mark and the capitalized *If* tell that the second sentence has a quotation.

I asked if the boys were in the bathtub.

He asked, "If the boys were in the bathtub, wouldn't it be fun to steal their towels?"

45. The second sentence makes sense only with quotations as shown.

I shouted Marla's last name to him.

I shouted, "Marla's last name is Jones!"

46. We know by the question mark that the second sentence has a quotation.

> We did not like what he asked.
> "We did not like what?" he asked.

47. Since Gardenia was asked about herself, *me* must refer to Gardenia in the first set, so Gardenia is speaking.

> I asked Gardenia how Ann felt about her. She said, "Ann is really mad at me."

In the second set *me* refers to the narrator, so there is no dialogue.

> I asked Gardenia how Ann felt about me. She said Ann is really mad at me.

Comma: Conjunctions—Tie It Up (pp. 19–21)

48. If the man were tall and skinny, the second part of the sentence would have to be separated as another sentence. We are told to use a comma; it makes sense that the two independent clauses are as shown below.

> The man was tall, and skinny dogs sniffed at him.

49. *Watch* is a noun *(ladies'* is possessive). No comma is needed.

> We sell the necklace and the ladies' watch. Only the buyer can see us.

50. *They* refers to the ladies (plural), and only the necklace is being sold. Each sentence has two independent clauses.

> We sell the necklace, and the ladies watch. They are hoping for a cheaper necklace, but this is our last item.

51. The noun *dogs* is plural and *run* is what they do; there are two independent clauses.

> The owners take off the collars, and the dogs run.

52. Since the dog is asleep, it can't be tagging. The word *tag* is a noun, not a verb, so no comma is needed.

> They take off the collar and the dog's tag. The dog never wakes up!

53. In sentence one, *two* refers to the pencils that were broken. The *two* in sentence three refers to the only tools NOT broken.

> We found all the pencils, but two were broken. We'd have to replace those two. We found that all the tools but two were broken. We kept those two good ones.

54. The first sentence has one subject with two verbs. In the second sentence, *Will* is a subject.

> The girls will dump the orange boots and will pick up green socks at the costume shop. They choose the masks, and Will picks the rubber noses.

55. The second sentence has two subjects, each with its own verb (*She / selects, others / plant*). The fourth sentence has one subject and verb (*we / see*).

> The queen begins the spring garden ceremony. She selects a bulb, and the others plant it.
> The two aliens show their homes. We see the one's star and the other's planet.

56. In the second sentence, *maple* is a subject and *leaves* is a verb. In the fourth sentence, *maple* is an adjective for the noun *leaves*.

> When do we get rid of our wood furniture? The oak goes now, and the maple leaves later.
> We will put off cleaning the yard. We will rake all the oak leaves and the maple leaves later.

57. In sentence one, *read* and *were* are past tense verbs. In sentence two, *we're (we are)* includes both a subject and a verb.

> Earlier, they read the book but were tired. Now we read the book, but we're bored.

58. In the first sentence, *headlights* is a noun. In the second sentence, *head* is a subject whose verb is *lights*.

> Take a look at the car and its headlights up in the distance.
> See the spaceship. Its tail blinks, and its head lights up in the distance.

Comma: Explain It (p. 22)

59. You speak to Grandma about the monkey. *A long attachment* explains *tail*.

> Grandma, the monkey is hanging upside down. It hangs by its tail, a long attachment.

60. You speak about Mrs. Greenfield, calling her *the old bat*.

> Watch out! Mrs. Greenfield, the old bat, is after you!
> You trampled those flowers, Mrs. Greenfield's pride and joy.

61. First, *a big surprise* is what you got your brother. Then, *a big surprise* explains what you got instead of a brother.

> I got my brother a big surprise. It was a new cell phone.

> I thought I'd get a new brother. Instead, I got a sister, a big surprise.

Question Mark/Period (pp. 23–24)

62. In the first sentence, *How* is the name of the boy (an answer to a question).

> How is the boy flying the hoverboard. That should answer your question. How many hovering tricks did you show him?

63. We know only that Dad picks spring clothes. Also, since there is no preposition, *May* indicates a question, not a month.

> February is the month when you pick our spring clothes, Dad. May we pick our summer clothes? In August, maybe we will pick fall clothes together.

64. The second sentence suggests that *do the desserts* is a command. The last sentence suggests that *do the desserts* is a question.

> When we have guests over, do the desserts last. That way, they'll be sure to eat the main course.

> When we have guests over, do the desserts last? If not, remember to make more next time!

65. a. *Will* and the second sentence suggest the first sentence is a question.

> Will the operas sound much better than last year? If not, I would rather stay home and listen to the dog howl.

b. The comma shows *Will* is a noun of address, so the first sentence, as well as the second, is a statement.

> Will, the operas sound better than last year. If they didn't, I would use my earplugs and read my book instead.

66. Sentence two suggests that sentence one is a question. Either a period or an exclamation mark is acceptable on sentence two.

> Do your brothers work? If the answer is no, you will have to do your brothers' work.

Exclamation Mark (pp. 25–26)

67. Adjectives in parentheses give hints.

> Tom (excited): Let's go see Liz wrestle that troll!

> Earl (bored): Go see it yourself.
> Lenny (scared): The trolls are coming here!
> Chloe (disbelieving): Sure, they're coming.

68. *Without interest* means there is no strong feeling.

> Without interest, Daryll read, "The tornado appeared suddenly from nowhere and picked up the whole house."

69. There is excitement, so ! is appropriate.

> Are you taking me to the rally tonight? I can't wait to see the monster trucks!

70. The context of surrounding sentences suggests the marks shown.

> **a.** If we win the lottery, we each get mucho bucks. What excitement!

> **b.** You say there's a lot of excitement going on down the street, but I can't see anything. What excitement?

> **c.** Oh boy, we get to hear another lecture. I think I'll take a nap. What excitement.

71. Word order suggests the sentence types.

> Did you really sneak out during Aunt Maude's visit? How rude that was!
> I didn't know it was rude to sneak out. How rude was that?

Apostrophe: Leaving Out Letters (p. 27)

72. *I'm* is a contraction for *I am*.

> I'm a pig owner. Ima Pig is the name of my pet.

73. The second *Well* is an introductory word. (*We will* makes no sense there.)

> We'll give you our best video games.
> Well, give them to us now!

74. The third *Weve* stands for *We have*. *He's* stands for *He is*.

> Jacob Weve, the stunt flyer, is coming! Weve has got to get ready to fly. He's letting us take his picture first. We've got to get ready for him!

75. Though the owner's name is *Shed*, only *She would* makes sense in sentence two.

> We know Eileen Shed, the owner of the skate park. She'd let us in for free if we asked!

Apostrophe: Who's An Owner 1 (pp. 28–29)

76. The first *sisters* is a plural noun, with *skate*

as the verb. The second *sisters* should be possessive, since it describes what is carried.

> She watches as her sisters skate down the hill. Oops! One of them loses a skate. <u>She finds and carries her sister's skate down the hill.</u>

77. The word *aunts* shows possession of the children (singular, as shown by *She*).

> My aunt's children are my cousins John and Paul. She lets them host their own website.

78. The first *boys* is a plural noun, as suggested by *they,* and *bat* is a verb. The second *boys* is singular, as suggested by *he,* and *bat* is a noun.

> The boys bat flies because they have no mosquitoes to practice on.
> The boy's bat flies because he swings it too hard and loses control!

79. In sentence one, *paint* is a verb. In sentence three, *TV* is a noun, so *uncles* is possessive (singular because of *his*).

> I come out to watch my friends paint over the wall. They are covering it well. I go back inside to watch my uncle's TV over his kitchen table.

Apostrophe: Who's An Owner 2 (pp. 30–31)

80. One sister would have only two eyes, so *sisters* must be a plural possessive.

> All of your sisters' eyes are like yours.

81. Sentence two shows *friends* is plural.

> Terry loves his friends' skateboards. Each friend has a board that is really fast.

82. The spellings of *babys* and *babies* show their number.

> At the wedding, there were beautiful flower arrangements of roses and baby's breaths. Too bad I had to leave early with the two sick babies. They just spit up again. Boy, these babies' breaths are stinky!

83. *That* indicates *cats* is singular. *Those* refers to all its claws.

> That cat's claws are sharp. Those claws' points can dig in!

84. The first *players* is a noun and *field* is a verb. The *field* in the last sentence is a noun, and *players* is possessive.

> The baseball players field drives. They do it well because the field they field on feels fairly flat. I can't field balls in our park. It's

too bumpy to catch even the balls right off the bat. Our baseball players' field drives me crazy.

85. The word *It* shows *nests* is a noun, so *squirrels* is possessive (and plural, as shown by *those*). *Familys* must be singular and possessive (or it would be *families*).

> I see those squirrels' nest. It has pictures hung around the inside edges. I thought they were the family's portraits, but now I see they are just nuts.

Quotation Marks: Quote or Title? (pp. 32–33)

86. The words *is* and *visual treat* suggest that *Apples* is a work of art (the picture on the right).

> "Apples" is a visual treat. The color is good, and the lines are neat.

> Bananas are a tasty treat. When I view art, they're good to eat!

87. *Caroline* is a girl; *Emeline* is art.

> Caroline is a fine example of a girl, but she's not inclined to spend her time in the modern art world.

> "Emeline" is a fine example of Impressionism, but I prefer the "Odyssey" as it's based on realism.

88. Context and the capital *C* suggest that the second *Hot Chocolate* is a song.

> Let's discuss our preferences over drinks. Hot chocolate is my favorite. Other drinks are okay, but this one is outstanding. It inspired Ricky to sing "Hot Chocolate" on karaoke night.

89. The first text in the quotation marks is a title, not something spoken word-for-word. *Clarence* must be separated from his quotation.

> Shanya read "The Rhino Blows His Own Horn," a poem about an overconfident rhinoceros.
> Clarence said, "The audience thought the rhino was too conceited."

90. The last sentence tells us that *Dancing* is a title. The last sentence makes sense only if the words *I am* are spoken.

> He wondered what she was doing next. She said "Dancing" was what she'd do next. "I thought you were going to do another song," he said.
> "I am," she said. "I just told you the title."